AF323069

THE MONEY GAME

DAVID ERICSON

A PACEMAKER® BOOK

Fearon/Janus/Quercus
Belmont, California

Simon & Schuster Education Group

The PACEMAKER BESTELLERS

Bestellers I

Diamonds in the Dirt
Night of the Kachina
The Verlaine Crossing
Silvabamba
The Money Game

Flight to Fear
The Time Trap
The Candy Man
Three Mile House
Dream of the Dead

Bestellers II

Black Beach
Crash Dive
Wind Over Stonehenge
Gypsy
Escape from Tomorrow

The Demeter Star
North to Oak Island
So Wild a Dream
Wet Fire
Tiger, Lion, Hawk

Bestellers III

Star Gold
Bad Moon
Jungle Jenny
Secret Spy
Little Big Top

The Animals
Counterfeit!
Night of Fire and Blood
Village of Vampires
I Died Here

Bestellers IV

Dares
Welcome to Skull Canyon
Blackbeard's Medal
Time's Reach
Trouble at Catskill Creek

The Cardiff Hill Mystery
Tomorrow's Child
Hong Kong Heat
Follow the Whales
A Changed Man

Series Director: Tom Belina

Designer: Richard Kharibian

Cover and Illustrations: Joe Cleary

ISBN 0–8224–5266–9
Library of Congress Card Number: 77–81593

Printed in the United States of America.

10 9 8 7 6 5
MA

CONTENTS

1 THE GAME 1

2 DOUBLE YOUR MONEY 8

3 IT'S A LONG STORY 13

4 I'LL SEE WHAT I CAN DO 19

5 THE SET UP 25

6 DIAMONDS IN HIS EYES 30

7 TWO BIRDS WITH ONE STONE 36

8 WHAT'S GOING ON HERE? 39

CHAPTER **1**

The Game

He woke up late in the morning. The sun was already high in the sky.

A new day, he thought. A new day in which to play the game. The thought made him feel good. He got out of bed and began to dress.

Soon he was ready—ready to play the game again. He went outside and walked down the street. He walked fast but not too fast. He wanted to see what there was to see. And who there was to see. You could never tell what you might see out here on the street. Or who you might meet. So he kept his eyes wide open.

His name was Ross Sanders. He looked like a nice country boy. But he wasn't. He had been born here in the city. And he was street smart. A person had to be street smart in the city. It was the best way to live the good life, too.

As he walked toward a fruit store, he saw a little kid. There was something about the kid. Ross didn't know what it was. Something about the way the kid looked all around him. Up the street. Down the street. Into the store.

Ross saw the kid reach out and grab an apple. The kid began to run.

So did Ross. He caught the kid and said, "Hand it over."

"Let me go!" the kid said. "Mind your own business, man!"

Ross forced the kid to go back to the store. The man who owned the store came outside.

"Is something wrong?" he asked Ross.

"Give it back," Ross said to the kid.

The kid gave the apple to the man.

"I saw him steal it," Ross said.

"Thank you," the man said. "Thank you very much. These kids! They will steal anything."

Ross let the kid go. The kid ran down the street and around the corner.

"Have something," the man said to Ross. "Take an orange. Or would you rather have an apple? Take either."

Ross took an apple. "Thank you," he said.

"Thank *you*," the man said.

Ross walked down the street feeling good. The day was a fine one and he was happy. He looked at the apple.

Something for nothing.

That was cool. But it wasn't really something for nothing. He had caught the kid. So the apple was his reward. Still it was all very cool, he thought.

He stopped at last in front of a small building. On the door was a sign. It said:

SENIOR CITIZENS' CENTER

He opened the door and went inside.

Inside were many people. Most of them were old. The young ones were volunteers at the Center. They helped the old people make things like baskets and art. They kept them company.

Just as Ross himself did.

"Ross!" someone said. It was an old man. "Come over here. I want to talk to you."

Ross waved to the man. But he didn't go over. He looked around the room. Finally he saw her. She was with another woman. Both of them had white hair. Both of them wore glasses.

He went to them. "Good morning," he said.

One woman put her arms around him. "Hello, dear," she said. "Oh, I'm so glad to see you. I thought maybe you wouldn't come today."

"I always come, Mrs. Drake," Ross said.

The woman said, "I've told you so many times." She shook a finger at him.

"Told me? Told me what?"

"Don't call me Mrs. Drake. You and I are friends. We have been for a long time. *Good* friends. So call me Sally."

"OK, Sally," Ross said with a smile.

The other woman smiled, too. "I'll see you later, Sally," she said. "Two is company but three is a crowd."

Sally and Ross laughed as the woman left them to talk to someone else.

"Come over here and sit down," Sally said to Ross. She took his hand and they went over to a little table by a window. "Would you like some coffee and cake?"

"I'll get it," Ross said. "You just sit right there. I'll be right back."

And he was. He brought with him two cups of coffee and two pieces of cake.

Sally drank some of her coffee. She ate a little bit of cake.

Ross watched her. He was waiting for her to say something. He was sure that she would. Finally she did.

"I've been thinking, Ross."

"You have? About what?"

"About what you said yesterday."

"You mean about how I can double your money for you?"

"Yes. But I'm still not sure what I should do. I really don't have very much money. And if something happened to it—"

"If you lost it," Ross said, "that would be bad. I understand that. That's why I told you to think over what I said yesterday."

"I *would* like to double my money," Sally said. "Everything costs so much these days. Clothes. Food. *Everything!*"

"I know," Ross said. He reached out and took Sally's hand in his. "Let me ask you something. You didn't tell anyone about what I said yesterday, did you?"

"Of course I didn't. Not a word. You made me promise not to."

"Good," Ross said. "I don't want too many people to know about it. It might spoil it for the rest of us."

"You said it would be a safe thing to do with my money," Sally said.

"It is safe, Sally. You can double your money in just a few days. That's a fact. If you don't believe me—"

"I do believe you, Ross. I guess I'm just afraid. I don't want anything to happen to the little money I have."

Ross still held Sally's hand. "I'll tell you what," he said to her. "How about this idea? I'll give you one thousand dollars of my own money. Then you give me one thousand dollars of your money. If I don't double your money, you keep mine."

"Oh, I couldn't do that," Sally said. "That wouldn't be fair."

"It will make you feel safe," Ross said. He put a hand in his pocket. He took out some money. He gave the money to Sally.

"Count it," he said.

Sally counted it. "One thousand dollars," she whispered.

"You keep it."

Sally didn't say anything for a minute. Then she said, "Let's get out of here."

"Where do you want to go?" Ross asked her.

"To my bank," she answered. "I'll take out my one thousand dollars. I'll give it to you."

She went to the door. Ross followed her. There was a big smile on his face. Sally didn't see it.

The game was beginning again. He liked to play it more than anything.

CHAPTER 2

DOUBLE YOUR MONEY

Ed Price came to the Senior Citizens' Center. He went inside and looked around.

He didn't see the person he was looking for.

A young woman came up to him. "Are you a volunteer here?" she asked Ed.

He shook his head.

"We are always in need of good volunteers," the woman said. "Do you want to be one?"

"No, thank you," Ed said. "I came here to look for my grandmother. Her name is Mrs. Drake. Mrs. Sally Drake. Is she here?"

"I don't believe she is," the woman said. "In fact, I think she left just a little while before you came."

"She did," a man near them said. "I saw her go. She left with Ross."

"Thank you," the woman said to the man.

To Ed, she said, "Ross Sanders is one of our volunteers. He sometimes takes our senior citizens out for walks. Or to the store to shop. He probably took your grandmother to shop. Ross is so good about things like that. We are really in luck to have him with us."

"Thank you," Ed said. He left the Center. He went to Sally's house to wait for her there.

He didn't have long to wait. In less than an hour, he saw Sally coming up the street.

When she saw Ed, she waved to him. When she reached him, she said, "Ed, I'm so glad to see you! Come inside and let's talk."

"I was supposed to meet you at the Center," Ed said as they went into the house.

"Oh, I forgot!" Sally said.

"That's OK," Ed said.

"Sit down," Sally said when they got to the kitchen. "How are you?"

"Fine," Ed said. "And how are *you*?"

"I'm fine, Ed. Just as fine as could be. In fact, I'm very happy. Do you want to know why?"

"Sure I do. What are you so happy about?"

Sally did a little dance in the middle of the kitchen. "Because," she said, "I will soon be a rich woman!"

Ed just looked at her. What, he wondered, was she talking about? He decided to wait. He knew his grandmother would tell him.

Sally sat down next to Ed. "I have a friend," she said to him. "His name is Ross Sanders. He is a volunteer at the Center. And he is so good to me—to all of us there. He is the one who is going to make me rich."

"How?"

"I don't really know *how*. But I know he will."

Ed gave his grandmother a worried look.

"Don't look at me like that, dear," Sally said to him. "There isn't a thing in the world to worry about."

"Tell me about this—about Ross Sanders," Ed said.

"Well," Sally said. "It's really very simple. I went to the bank. I took out one thousand dollars. I gave the money to Ross. In a few days, he is going to give me back two thousand dollars! Isn't that just *great?*"

"How is he going to do that?"

"You mean double my money?"

"Yes, that's what I mean."

"I told you I don't know how. I just know he is going to do it."

"I think you have made a mistake," Ed told his grandmother. "A big mistake."

"Oh, don't be silly, dear. Are you sure you don't want something to eat?"

Ed shook his head. "It was a mistake to give money to a stranger."

"A stranger? Ross isn't a stranger. He is a friend of mine. A very good friend. He wants to help make me rich."

"I don't believe it," Ed said. "I don't think you will ever see your money again. Or Ross Sanders either."

"Of course I will," Sally said.

"What makes you so sure?"

"This," Sally said. She showed Ed the money Ross had given her.

"Where did you get this?" he asked her. "I thought you said—"

"*This,*" said Sally, "is Ross' money. You see, I wasn't sure I should give him my money. So he wanted me to feel safe. He said if he didn't double my money, I could keep this—*his* money. That way I wouldn't be out a penny. Now what do you say to that?"

Ed, at first, didn't know what to say. Maybe his grandmother was right. Maybe everything would be OK. Didn't she have one thousand dollars right there in her hand?

"I guess I really should mind my own business," Ed said.

Sally gave him a smile. "I don't mind what you said. Not a bit. It shows that you care about me—about what happens to me. That's a very nice thing to know. It makes a person feel good to know that someone cares about them."

"I do care about you," Ed said. "I know how hard things have been for you. But if you say Ross Sanders is OK, well then—"

Sally gave Ed a kiss. "Please don't worry about me," she said.

"OK, I won't." Ed knew that what he had said was a lie. Because he did worry about his grandmother. And about this Ross Sanders. And about the one thousand dollars his grandmother had given Ross.

Sally was saying something. What was it? Ed listened.

"—and part of the one thousand dollars I gave Ross was for my rent. But soon I'll have *two* thousand dollars. I won't have to worry at all about the rent. Instead, I think I'll go out and buy myself a new dress!"

CHAPTER 3

It's a Long Story

Several days later, there was a knock on Sally's door.

She went to it and opened it. Ross Sanders stood outside.

"Ross!" she said. "Where have you been? I haven't seen you at the Center. Not since—"

"Not since the day you and I went to your bank," Ross said.

"And I gave you my money," Sally added.

"May I come in?"

"Of course. Come right in. Sit down. Can I get you something?"

"A cup of coffee would be nice," Ross said as he sat down.

Sally went into the kitchen to make coffee. Her heart was in her mouth. Did Ross have her money? Did he really double it as he said he would do? What if he had lost it? She almost spilled the cup of coffee she brought to Ross.

"This is good," he said as he tasted it. "Really good. Now then."

"Yes?"

"I've brought your money," Ross said. He put his hand in one of his pockets.

Sally wanted to ask him how much money he had brought. One thousand dollars? Two thousand?

But she didn't dare. She watched Ross' hand. It came out of his pocket. It was full of money. He handed the money to her.

"Count it," he said.

Sally did. She looked up at Ross. "I can't believe it," she said. "Is it really true?"

"It's true," Ross told her. "There are two thousand dollars there."

"How ever did you do it?" Sally asked him.

"It's a long story," Ross answered. "Do you really want me to explain it all to you?"

Sally shook her head. "No, I guess I don't. I was never very good with money. I probably wouldn't understand a word you said. I'm just glad that you *did* do it. How you did it doesn't matter to me. Just as long as you didn't break any laws."

Ross finished his coffee. "I've got to go to the Center."

"If you will wait a minute or two, I'll go with you," Sally said.

"I've got some things to do first," Ross said. "I'll see you there later, OK?"

"Fine," Sally said. "See you later."

"Oh, one thing," Ross said.

"Yes?"

"*My* money."

"Oh, I'm so sorry," Sally said. "I forgot all about it. I'll get it for you right now."

She rushed from the room. She was back in a minute. In her hand was the thousand dollars Ross had given her.

She handed it to him. "Thank you, dear," she said. She gave him a quick kiss. "Thank you ever so much. You have been so very good to me. Just like a son."

She was about to give Ross another kiss. But he walked to the door.

"Good-bye," he said.

"Until later," Sally said. "At the Center."

He waved and was gone.

Sally closed the door behind him. She sat down. She counted the money again.

It was really true! Her one thousand dollars had turned into two thousand dollars.

Now she wouldn't have to worry about how to pay her rent. She was in good shape for a long time to come.

It was then that the thought crossed her mind. If Ross could double her money once, she thought, he could do it twice. But would he? Of course he would, she decided. She would ask him. All he could do was say yes or no.

She changed her clothes. Then she left for the Center.

The first thing she did when she got there was to look for Ross. But she didn't see him. She asked several people if they had seen him.

They told her that he had not been at the Center all day.

Sally decided that he must be busy. Soon he would come to the Center, she thought.

But she was wrong. Ross did not come to the Center that day.

Finally, Sally gave up on him. She would see him tomorrow. She left the Center.

On her way home, she remembered that she wanted to buy a new dress.

When she came to a dress shop near her home, she went inside.

A woman showed her several dresses. Sally finally picked one. It was blue and white. It had a little bit of yellow at the neck.

"It looks very good on you," the woman told Sally. "Like it was made for you."

Sally smiled. She thought the dress made her look nice.

The woman packed the dress in a box. Sally gave her some money to pay for it.

The woman looked at the money Sally had given her. "Could you wait a minute, please?" she said.

"Yes, I can," Sally said. "But why? Is something wrong?"

"I'll be right back," the woman said. She turned and went into the back of the store.

When she came back a minute later, there was a man with her.

"This is Mr. Cole," the woman said. "He owns the store."

"I'm very sorry," Mr. Cole said to Sally. "This money is not any good."

"Not any good?" Sally said. "Why what do you mean?"

"It's counterfeit," Mr. Cole said.

Sally couldn't speak.

"Of course, I'm sure you didn't know it was counterfeit," Mr. Cole said.

"I didn't," Sally whispered. "Please believe me. I thought it was good money."

"I'm sure you did," Mr. Cole said. "Perhaps you have some other money you can use to pay for the dress?"

"Oh, yes," Sally said, "I do have some. Here." She gave Mr. Cole some money.

He held it up to the light and looked at it. "This is counterfeit too, I'm afraid."

Sally showed him all of the two thousand dollars she had.

"I'm sorry," Mr. Cole said. "*All* of this money is counterfeit."

CHAPTER **4**

I'll See What I Can Do

Sally walked slowly out of the store—without the dress.

She went down the street. People passed her. She didn't even see them.

She started to cross the street. A car almost hit her because she had crossed when the light was red.

Finally, she got home. She went into her house and sat down. She wondered what she should do. Should she go to the Center and try to find Ross? But the Center was closed now.

Should she go there tomorrow? Maybe someone had given Ross the counterfeit money. Maybe he didn't know it was counterfeit. She made up her mind. She would talk to him tomorrow.

She went to bed. But she couldn't sleep. She lay awake almost all night long.

In the morning, she couldn't eat breakfast. She wasn't a bit hungry. She put on her coat and went to the Center.

Ross wasn't there.

She waited all day for him. But he didn't come. It was then that she knew he had tricked her. She felt as if she were going to cry. But she forced herself not to.

She got up to leave the Center. As she did so, someone came in the door. It was her grandson, Ed Price.

When Sally saw him, she wanted to hide. How could she face him? What would he say to her when he found out what had happened?

Ed saw Sally. He came over to her. "I thought I'd find you here. How are you?"

"I'd like to go home now," Sally told him.

Ed knew at once that something was wrong. But he didn't ask Sally what it was. Instead, he walked her home. On the way, he talked. But Sally didn't say much.

When they got to her house, they went inside.

Ed said, "Something is wrong, isn't it?"

In a low voice, Sally said, "Yes, something is very wrong."

"Is it about the money?" Ed asked her. "The money you gave to Ross Sanders?"

Sally said that it was. Then she told him what had happened the day before.

"I'm sorry about what happened," Ed said. "I really am. But I'm not at all surprised."

"I should not have given him my money," Sally said. "You were right. I was wrong. I'm just an old fool."

"No, you're not a fool," Ed said. "You're just a nice person who believes other people are all nice, too. That's the real mistake you made. You think everyone is as good a person as you are. Well, I can tell you that they are not. Not all of them."

"What am I going to do?" Sally asked Ed. "How can I get my money back? *Is* there any way to get it back?"

"Maybe I can help," Ed said. "I'll try to find Ross. If I do—" He said no more.

"Would you help me?" Sally said. "I really need that money. I have to pay my rent in two weeks and—"

"Try not to worry," Ed told her. "I'll see what I can do. I'll get on it right away. I'll be in touch."

He left the house. He wasn't sure what—if anything—he could do. But he was going to try to get his grandmother's money back.

He went to his friend's house. His friend's name was Bill Evans. Bill was home and he listened to Ed's story.

"That sure is some rip-off," Bill said when Ed had finished. "That Ross Sanders should be in jail. Let's go to the police and—"

"No," Ed said. "I don't want to go to the police. I did think about going to them. But I decided not to."

"Why?" Bill asked.

"Because, even if the police get Ross, my grandmother probably won't get any of her money back."

"You think he has spent it already?"

"Probably."

"What can we do then?" Bill asked.

"I'm not sure just yet," Ed said. "But I do have one idea."

"An idea?"

"I don't want to tell you about it now. First we have to try to find Ross. If we do, then I'll tell you about my idea."

"I don't know what he looks like," Bill said.

"I don't either, come to think of it. Let's go and talk to my grandmother. She can tell us what he looks like."

Ed and Bill went to Sally's house.

"Can you tell us what Ross looks like?" Ed asked his grandmother.

"I can do better than that," Sally answered. "I have a picture of him. I'll get it for you."

When Sally came back with the picture, she gave it to Ed.

The picture showed Sally and a man with dark hair standing in front of the Center. They were both smiling.

"So this is Ross Sanders," Ed said. He gave the picture to Bill to look at. To Sally, he said, "Can we keep this picture?"

"Yes," Sally said. "I don't ever want to see Ross Sanders' face again."

Ed and Bill left the house.

"Let's get something to eat," Bill said. "I'm hungry."

They went into a place and ate.

Bill took some money from his pocket. He gave it to a man to pay for their food.

The man looked at the money.

"Is something wrong?" Bill asked him.

The man shook his head. "No, nothing wrong. This money is OK. But I have to be careful. A lot of counterfeit money has been passed around here."

The man gave Bill his change. He and Ed left the store.

Outside, Ed said, "I bet I know where all the counterfeit money is coming from."

"From Ross Sanders?"

"Right. He may have done to other old people what he did to my grandmother. And if that's true, then I think I know where we might find him."

"Me too," Bill said. "Where there are other old people. At other Senior Citizens' Centers here in the city."

"Let's check them out," Ed said.

Ed and Bill went to a Senior Citizens' Center. It was on the other side of the city. Just as they got near it, Bill said, "Look over there—across the street."

Ed looked. Then he said, "That's him! That's Ross Sanders!"

"He looks just like his picture," Bill said.

They watched Ross cross the street. They saw him go into the Center.

"Come on," Ed said. "Let's go in there."

They went inside the Center.

"There he is," Bill whispered to Ed. "Over there in the corner with that old man."

"Can I help you?" asked a woman.

"Yes," Ed said, "you can. My friend and I were thinking we might like to help out here. But first we thought we would like to take a look around."

"Fine," the woman said. "I'll have someone show you around the Center. I'll ask one of our volunteers." She went away. She came back with Ross Sanders.

"This is Ross," she said to Ed and Bill. "He is one of our volunteers. And a very good one. Ross has only been with us for a few days. But he can show you around, I'm sure."

"Hello there," Ross said.

Ed and Bill told Ross their names. Then Ross took them around the Center. He showed them what volunteers do.

"It's not hard work," he said. "In fact, it's fun. You get to meet a lot of nice people. You get a chance to help them out. Helping people is the best part of the job."

Ed looked at Bill. But he didn't say anything.

Ross took them to meet some of the people at the Center.

After a little while, Ed and Bill went back to the woman they had met before.

"We would like to be volunteers," Ed said.

"Very good," said the woman. "When can you come here to help us?"

"What time does Ross work here?" Ed asked.

"He could sort of teach us what to do," Bill said. "Until we get the hang of it."

The woman told them when Ross was at the Center. Ed and Bill said they would come at the same time.

"When can you start working?" the woman asked them.

"Tomorrow," Ed said.

"Fine," the woman said, with a smile. "See you tomorrow then."

Outside, Ed said to Bill, "Well, we did it. We found him."

"Now what?" Bill said.

"Now we have to get some help from my grandmother. And from her friends. That is, if we can."

They went to Sally's house.

She was glad to see them. She asked them if they had found Ross Sanders. They told her that they had.

"Now what are you going to do?" she asked.

"I have an idea," Ed said. "I think I know how to get your money back."

He told Sally and Bill about his idea.

"But for that idea to work," Sally said, "you would need a lot of money."

"That's where you come in," Ed told her.

"But I haven't any more money," Sally said. "How can I help you?"

"Talk to your friends at the Center," Ed said. "Tell them what Ross did to you. Ask them to help us."

Sally said she would do it.

Ed and Bill left.

The next day, Sally telephoned Ed. "I've got some money," she told him. She told him how much she had. "Seven of my friends each gave me some," she said. "Is it enough?"

"Yes, it's enough," Ed said. "I'll come over and get it."

On the way to Sally's house, Ed stopped for his friend Bill. Then the two of them went to meet with Sally.

She gave them the money. "I do hope your plan works out," she said.

"So do I," Ed said. "It's worth a try."

Then Ed and Bill left Sally. They went to a building in the center of the city.

Ed bought several kinds of diamonds.

Then he and Bill went to the Center and began to work. They were there for only a few minutes when Ross came in.

Later, Ed went and stood next to Ross. There were no other people near them.

Ed let a little bag fall out of his pocket. The bag hit the floor. Out of it fell some diamonds.

"You dropped something," Ross said. He was about to pick up the bag. But instead he just stood there. He looked down at the diamonds on the floor.

Ed got down on the floor. He picked up the diamonds. He put them back in the bag. He put the bag back in his pocket.

"Were those diamonds?" Ross asked him.

"Yes, they were," Ed said. He walked away.

Ross ran after him. "Were they real? Where did you get them?"

"Maybe I'll tell you some time," Ed said. "And maybe I won't."

"Come on, man!" Ross said. "Tell me!"

But Ed wouldn't.

CHAPTER 6

DIAMONDS IN HIS EYES

Ed and Bill worked at the Center for another hour. All during that time, Ross kept after Ed.

He wanted to know about the diamonds.

Ed told him nothing at first. But then he did answer some of Ross' questions.

"Where did they come from?" Ross asked.

"From a friend of mine," Ed answered.

"What are you going to do with them?"

"Sell them."

"Are they worth a lot of money?"

Ed smiled. "You saw them. What do you think?"

"I think they could make a man rich," Ross said. There was a funny look in his eyes.

"You know something?" Ed said. "You're right. They could make a man *very* rich."

"How did your friend get the diamonds?" Ross asked. "Did he give them to you? Or did you buy them from him?"

Ed wouldn't answer any more questions.

So Ross went to Bill. He asked Bill his questions.

Bill seemed to be glad to answer them.

He told Ross what Ed had told him to say.

He told Ross that the diamonds had been stolen in France. He said that Ed had bought them from the man who had stolen them. He said that Ed was going to sell them. He would get a lot more money than he had paid for them.

"So you two are in this diamond game together?" Ross asked Bill.

Bill said they were.

Ross didn't say anything more.

But the next day he talked to Ed at the Center. "Your friend told me about the diamonds yesterday," he said. "You're pretty smart, you two."

"I'll kill him!" Ed said. "I told Bill not to tell anyone about them," he lied.

"Don't be mad," Ross said. "I won't tell anyone. Not unless—"

Ed looked at him. "Not unless what?"

"Not unless," Ross said, "you don't let me in on your game."

"No way!" Ed said. "No way in the world!"

"OK," Ross said. "OK." He began to smile. "But someone just might tell the police about you two."

"By someone I suppose you mean Ross Sanders."

"I do."

Ed thought for a minute. "OK," he said at last. "I guess you've got me. Thanks to Bill and his big mouth. You're in."

Ross held out his hand.

Ed shook it.

"I want to buy some of those diamonds," Ross said. He told Ed what he would pay for them.

"But that's less than *I* paid for them!"

"That's my price," Ross said. "Take it—or take the police on your tail."

Ed went into an empty room. Ross followed him into it. Ed gave Ross a few of the diamonds.

"Now give me the money," Ed said.

"Not yet. Not until I make sure these diamonds are real."

"Well, I guess that's only fair," Ed said.

They left the Center. They went to the building where Ed had bought the diamonds.

People in the building were in the business of buying and selling diamonds.

Ross paid a man to tell him if the diamonds were real. The man said they were.

Later, outside the building, Ross gave Ed some money.

"Now it's my turn," Ed said.

"What do you mean?"

Ed explained. "There has been a lot of counterfeit money passed in the city. I want to make sure this money is the real thing. Let's go to a bank."

"Wait a minute," Ross said. "I can spot counterfeit money. Let me see the money I just gave you."

Ed gave it to him. Ross looked at it. "Well," Ross said. "What do you know? This money *is* counterfeit! Someone must have slipped it to me and I didn't even know it. But don't worry. I have more money at home. Good money."

Ed went to Ross' house. Ross gave Ed some different money.

"I still want to check it out at a bank," Ed said. "I want to make sure."

They went to a bank. The woman in the bank said the money wasn't counterfeit.

"So long," Ed said to Ross outside the bank.

"Wait a minute. We aren't finished with our business yet."

"What do you mean?" Ed asked.

"Just this," Ross said. "Next time you make a buy, I want in."

"No," Ed said. "Not a second time. I can't make any money with you."

"You can't make any money if you end up in jail either," Ross said.

"You win," Ed said. "I'm going to make another buy tomorrow. And those diamonds will be worth a lot more than the ones I just sold you."

Ed told Ross how much the diamonds would cost him.

At first, Ross said he wouldn't pay that much. But Ed just smiled.

"You will," Ed said, "or you won't get even one diamond."

"The police—" Ross began.

"I'll take my chances," Ed said. "They will have to catch me first. I don't think they will."

Ross gave in. He said he would raise the money.

"I'll meet you at the Center tomorrow," he said. "When will you have the diamonds?"

"By seven o'clock tomorrow night," Ed said. "I'll meet you then."

They parted.

Ed went to Bill's house. He told him what had just happened. "And he was going to pass me some of his counterfeit money," Ed said to his friend. "He must think I don't know my way around."

Bill slapped Ed on the back. "You did it!" he yelled. "Good for you, man!"

"I did it—so far. But it's not all over yet. It won't be until after tomorrow night."

"I'd better go with you tomorrow night," Bill said. "Just in case you need some help."

"Thanks. I may need some help," Ed said. "With someone like Ross, who knows?"

CHAPTER 7

TWO BIRDS WITH ONE STONE

The next morning Ed went to the police to ask for help for the people at the Senior Citizens' Centers. People like his grandmother.

He spoke to a policeman at a desk in the police station.

"A man took some money from my grandmother," he said. "He said he was going to double it. But he gave her back counterfeit money."

"I've heard of that rip-off," the policeman said.

Ed said, "Money has been stolen from a lot of old people. A lot of them are getting beat up, too. I work at one of the Centers as a volunteer. I thought maybe one of your men could come there. Maybe he would tell the people there how to keep themselves and their money safe."

"I can send someone to your Center," the policeman said. "When do you want him?"

"Would tomorrow be OK?"

"What time tomorrow?"

"Three o'clock."

"OK," the policeman said. "Three it is."

"Thank you," Ed said. He thought, I've just made sure I will kill two birds with one stone.

He still had a lot of time before he was supposed to meet Ross. So he went to visit his grandmother.

He told her what had happened so far. He also told her what would happen at seven o'clock that night. And about his visit to the police. He asked her to come and listen to the policeman.

Sally asked him if he wasn't afraid of Ross.

Ed said he wasn't.

"I hope everything will be OK," Sally said. "I don't want you to get hurt."

"Will you come to the Center where I work then?" he asked. "At three o'clock tomorrow afternoon?"

Sally said she would be there.

"See you later," Ed said and left.

He went to Bill's house. Then he and Bill went to the Center.

They got there at five minutes before seven o'clock. Ross was already there.

"Have you got the diamonds?" he asked Ed.

"I've got them."

"Come on in here then," Ross said.

They went into an empty room.

"Have *you* got the money?" Bill asked him.

Ross put it on the table.

Then Ed put a little bag on the table. Bill counted the money. Ross opened the bag.

"Beautiful," he said. "These diamonds are really beautiful!"

"Let's go," Ed said to Bill. He started toward the door. Bill was right behind him.

"I'm going to be here at three tomorrow," he said. "I'll see you here then, Bill."

"Tomorrow at three," Bill said.

Ross heard what they had said as he put the diamonds back in the bag. He put the bag in his pocket. Then he left the room and the Center.

Ed and Bill looked at one another.

"I think we should go, too," Bill said.

"Yes," Ed said. "I don't want to see Ross again—not before three o'clock tomorrow."

"*Will* we see him then?"

"I'm sure we will," Ed said. "Yes, we will see him tomorrow. Mark my words."

CHAPTER 8

WHAT'S GOING ON HERE?

Next day, Ed got to the Center a few minutes before three o'clock. Bill was with him.

They went inside and looked around.

"Ross isn't here," Bill said.

"He will be," Ed said. "Don't worry about it."

Just then a man Ed had never seen before came in. He walked up to Ed.

"I'm Detective Thomas," he said. "I'm supposed to talk to the people here."

"Nice to meet you," Ed said. "My name is Ed Price. I'm the one who asked the police to send someone here."

"I'm all set to go," Detective Thomas said. "Do you want me to begin now?"

"Sure," Ed said. "Come on up to the front of the room."

Ed asked everyone to listen to him. He told them who Detective Thomas was. He told them why he had come to talk to them.

The people in the Center got chairs. They all sat down. Detective Thomas stood in the front of the room. He began to talk to them.

Ed listened. Detective Thomas told the people how they could keep themselves safe on the street. He also told them how to keep their homes safe.

Suddenly, Bill grabbed Ed's arm. "There he is," he whispered.

Ed looked toward the door. Ross had just come in. He was looking around the room.

When he saw Ed, he came over to him.

"That was some rip-off you pulled on me last night," he said to Ed.

"Rip-off?" Ed said. "What do you mean?"

Before Ross could say anything, Sally walked in the door.

When Ross saw her, he said, "In here, you two. Move!"

He pushed Ed and Bill into an empty room, as Sally sat down. She didn't see them.

"Those diamonds were not even worth a hundred dollars," Ross said.

"Really?" said Ed.

Ross grabbed him. "I want my money back. And I want it fast. If I don't get it, you and your friend will—"

"Get out of here!" Bill said to Ross.

"You're not going to get your money back," Ed said. "Get going."

"That's what you think!" Ross said. He suddenly hit Ed.

Ed fell back against the wall.

Bill jumped Ross.

Ross let out a yell. He shook Bill off his back. Then he made a grab for Ed.

He caught him. He hit him again. This time Bill let out a yell.

And then a second yell.

Ed hit Ross once, twice. Ross fell to the floor.

But he was on his feet again right away. The fight went on. During it, Bill let out several more yells.

Suddenly, the door of the room flew open.

Detective Thomas ran into the room. "What's going on in here anyway?" he shouted. *"Cut it out!"*

"Get out of here!" Ross yelled at him. "Mind your own business."

Ross hit Ed again.

Detective Thomas grabbed Ross and held his arms. Ross couldn't move.

"Get your hands off me!" Ross said, trying to break free. *"Let me go!"*

"What is this fight all about?" Detective Thomas asked Ed.

"I'm sorry, Detective Thomas," Ed said. "We were—"

Ross said, "Detective Thomas? You're a *detective?*"

"I am," said Detective Thomas. "Who are you? What's your name?"

Just then Sally came to the door with some other people. "I can tell you who he is!" she said. "He makes counterfeit money. His name is Ross Sanders!"

"What is this about counterfeit money?" Detective Thomas asked Sally.

She told him what Ross had done to her.

When she finished, Ross said, "Those two guys—they sold me stolen diamonds. But the diamonds were worth next to nothing. They—"

"Is that true?" Detective Thomas asked.

"It's true that we sold him some diamonds," Bill said.

"But," Ed said, "the diamonds were not stolen. I bought them. See this paper?" He gave a sales slip to Detective Thomas. It showed that Ed had bought the diamonds.

"Can I tell this nice Detective the rest of the story?" Sally asked.

"Sure," Ed said. "Go ahead."

Sally told Detective Thomas what Ed and Bill had done. They bought the diamonds, she said. Then they made believe that the diamonds were stolen. Ross wanted some of the diamonds so he could make money on them. Sally said that Ed and Bill gave him some good diamonds the first time.

"But the second time," she said, "Ed gave Ross different diamonds. *Those* diamonds were worth only a little money."

"But I paid him a *lot* for them!" Ross yelled.

"There is nothing against the law in what they did," Detective Thomas said to Ross. "They had diamonds for sale. You bought them. That's that."

"It was a rip-off!" Ross yelled.

"Yes," Ed said, "it was. But it wasn't against the law."

Detective Thomas let Ross go. "Don't move," he told him. He took everything out of Ross' pockets.

He found some money in one of Ross' pockets. He took a close look at it.

"This is counterfeit money," he said.

"See!" Sally said. "I told you!"

"Come on," Detective Thomas said to Ross.

"Where?" Ross asked.

"To the police station," Detective Thomas said. He took him from the Center.

"Well!" said Sally. "Didn't this turn out to be some afternoon?"

"And it's not over yet," Ed said. He gave one thousand dollars to Sally. "Now you have your money back."

"Oh, thank you," Sally said. She gave Ed a big kiss. Then she gave one to Bill, too.

"And here is the rest of it," Ed said. "This money is what you got from your friends so we could buy the diamonds."

"Good!" Sally said, taking the money. "Now I can pay them all back."

When she had left the room, Ed still had some money in his hand. He gave half of it to Bill. He kept the other half.

"What do we do with this?" Bill asked.

"Anything we want," Ed said. "You heard what Detective Thomas said. We didn't do anything wrong. So the money that's left over is ours, right? Let's go out and spend it."

"I do need some new clothes," Bill said. "And a new pair of shoes and—"

"So let's go," Ed said, "before the money burns a hole in your pocket."